# The Long Trip Home

by Helena Strong
illustrated by Lyuba Bogan

Scott Foresman
is an imprint of

Glenview, Illinois • Boston, Massachusetts • Chandler, Arizona
Upper Saddle River, New Jersey

**Illustrator** Lyuba Bogan

**Photographs**
Every effort has been made to secure permission and provide appropriate credit for photographic material. The publisher deeply regrets any omission and pledges to correct errors called to its attention in subsequent editions.

Unless otherwise acknowledged, all photographs are the property of Pearson Education, Inc.

Photo locators denoted as follows: Top (T), Center (C), Bottom (B), Left (L), Right (R), Background (Bkgd)

**24** Michael P. Gadomski/SuperStock

ISBN 13: 978-0-328-52057-2
ISBN 10:     0-328-52057-8

1 2 3 4 5 6 7 8 9 10 V0G1 13 12 11 10 09

J ake and his teammates traded high fives on the soccer field. The decisive victory against the first-place Panthers was a huge upset, but Jake didn't feel much like celebrating.

He wished his parents had been there. But they both had to work late at the hospital in Bangor yet again. To Jake, it seemed like his parents were missing more and more of his games. At least Uncle Dave had been there to see him score the winning goal.

Jake spotted his uncle making his way through the crowd onto the field. "Great game, Jake," Uncle Dave said, throwing an arm around Jake's shoulder. "We'd better get going. It's getting late, and it looks like there could be another downpour any minute."

Jake grabbed his backpack and followed his uncle to his station wagon. Once inside, Jake took off his pads and cleats and put on his sneakers. He wished he had thought of packing a clean, dry sweatshirt this morning. His jersey was muddy and damp from playing on the rain-soaked field.

"You must be starving," Uncle Dave said as he pulled out of the school parking lot and turned down the road that led out to his house in rural Maine. "I made some stew for dinner. It's all ready for us when we get home."

"I really thought Mom and Dad would be here this time," Jake grumbled.

"I know they would have been here if they could. Your dad said they would be able to make the next one," Uncle Dave said, trying to stay neutral.

"I've heard that before," Jake said under his breath.

Lately, he'd been spending a lot of time at Uncle Dave's house in the country. His uncle was a writer. He worked from home, so he was able to watch Jake when his parents had to work long hours at the hospital. And he always tried to make it fun. They normally ate their dinner over a game of chess and then watched their favorite TV shows until his parents came to pick him up.

"Got a lot of homework tonight?" Uncle Dave asked.

"Some math and history—not too much," Jake answered.

"So I'll have plenty of time to beat you in chess," Uncle Dave said with a smile.

Jake knew that Uncle Dave was intentionally trying to cheer him up, but his jokes weren't going to work tonight. Not only was Jake angry about his parents missing another important game, but he was also tired, cold, and sopping wet.

Uncle Dave turned onto a back road that led to his house. The road was narrow and dark. Pine trees like sentinels blocked out the dimming light.

"It's getting darker earlier and earlier," Uncle Dave remarked.

Jake noticed that he couldn't see anything past the car's headlights. He never felt really safe traveling on these back roads, especially at night. The woods were a playground for coyotes, bobcats, and black bears. Jake wasn't fond of wild animals. He didn't even like crossing paths with a harmless white-tailed deer.

It started to rain, and Uncle Dave turned on the windshield wipers. He instinctively leaned forward to see the road more clearly and didn't speak as he drove down the slick, winding road.

Jake shivered.

"It won't be too long now," Uncle Dave said, a bit too cheerily.

Just then, the station wagon drove through a large puddle. Water sprayed up and covered the windshield, blocking their already limited visibility. Uncle Dave gasped. The car hydroplaned for several seconds before he was able to get it back under control. Jake gripped the door handle and clenched his jaw. He didn't want Uncle Dave to know he was scared.

Jake sat forward in his seat, trying to make out familiar landmarks that signaled Uncle Dave's road, but he could hardly see anything. They were both silent as they listened to the pounding of the rain on the car's roof and the steady beat of the windshield wipers.

Suddenly, Jake locked eyes with a large deer, frozen in the car's headlights.

"Watch out!" Jake shouted.

Uncle Dave swerved onto the shoulder and just missed the stag.

The station wagon barreled forward in the direction of the woods. Jake covered his eyes just before the impact. He heard the crunch of metal as the front of the car was compressed against the tree. His body jerked forward, and his seatbelt pulled him back. Jake uncovered his eyes and looked over at his uncle. His head was resting on the steering wheel.

"Uncle Dave?" There was no response. "Uncle Dave?" he called out insistently. "Are you okay?"

Uncle Dave slowly lifted his head from the wheel and turned to Jake. "I think so. What about you?"

"Yeah, yeah, I'm okay," Jake said.

"That was really scary. The car looks pretty banged up," said Uncle Dave.

"What are we going to do?"

"We'll have to walk to my house."

"Shouldn't we stay with the car and wait for help?" Jake asked, trying to remember what he'd been told to do in an emergency. He also knew that the last thing he wanted to do was walk along this back road at night.

"Not many cars travel on this road," Uncle Dave explained. "Our best bet is to go into the woods a little ways and then take the old service road. It's a straight shot to my house from there, so it shouldn't take more than an hour or so."

Still shaken from the crash, Jake took out his cell phone, thinking he'd call his parents for help. Suddenly he missed them, even though they'd missed his game. "We'll never get cell phone service out here," Uncle Dave said.

Jake flipped open his phone anyway and saw that his uncle was right. He looked out his window. "It's just so creepy out here," Jake said, his voice trembling involuntarily.

"We'll be fine, but if it makes you feel any better, take this." Uncle Dave turned to the back seat of the station wagon and drew out an industrial flashlight.

Jake took the flashlight and stepped out into the pouring rain. Uncle Dave took the keys out of the ignition and joined his nephew beside the damaged car.

"Just stay right next to me and you'll be fine," Uncle Dave reassured him.

They slowly made their way through the thick brush. Jake could hardly see anything beyond the flashlight's beam; he matched his uncle's pace, step for step.

Eventually, the forest opened onto a ribbon of gravel and grass. They had reached the service road.

"How do you know the service road will take us to your house?" Jake asked skeptically.

"Because I walk the dogs here all the time."

"Not when it's pitch black though," Jake said.

"I know it looks scary, but it'll be fine," Uncle Dave reassured him.

Jake blindly looked around and imagined the wild animals that lurked in the darkness. He began to shake, both from fear and from the dropping temperature.

"You must be freezing," said Uncle Dave. He took off his jacket and handed it to Jake. "Here. This might help."

The rain slowed to a drizzle. "What a perfect night for a stroll in the woods," Uncle Dave joked. "My dogs would be so jealous if they knew about this."

"Very funny, Uncle Dave."

And then, Jake heard a sound —a rustling, growling, snorting, howling sound. Jake reflexively grabbed his uncle's arm. His mind raced. *There's something out there...wolves...coyotes....What is that?*

"Uncle Dave?" he whispered.

Uncle Dave hesitated. "I'm sure it's nothing," he said. "Let's just keep moving. We're almost there."

Jake would have broken into a sprint if he could have seen more than two feet in front of him. He took a deep breath and focused on each step, inching slightly closer to his uncle.

Uncle Dave started talking. "There's nothing out here that's going to hurt you. Walking on this road is safer than traveling on a freeway. I mean, obviously, you're safer walking here than driving home in my car tonight!"

Jake grinned at his uncle's attempt to calm him down. *Uncle Dave was probably right*, Jake told himself. His parents were always talking about the need to be careful on the road. They reminded him of this every time there was a news story about an accident, especially when it involved young people.

To keep his mind off his fear, Jake tried to picture the beautiful Maine woods in the sunlight on a spring afternoon. His parents had taken him hiking last spring, and he'd really enjoyed it. The trail had been wide and lined with wildflowers—not a wild animal in sight. *That was hiking,* he thought. *This is a nightmare.*

Now Jake noticed how hungry he was. He hadn't eaten for hours, not since his snack of juice and a granola bar before the soccer game. His mouth watered and his stomach growled as he thought about the dinner waiting for him on his uncle's stove.

"You know what? I almost forgot about these crackers I have in my pocket," Uncle Dave said.

He pulled out the package, opened it, and handed all four crackers to Jake.

Jake ate them slowly, relishing each bite. A break in the clouds allowed a half-moon to peek through. Jake and his uncle stopped short. They could see the moon's reflection in water that stretched in front of them. "What are we going to do *now?*" Jake asked.

"Take off our shoes and keep walking," Uncle Dave said matter-of-factly. "It's not deep."

"How do you know?" Jake asked.

"The water wasn't here when I walked the dogs the day before yesterday," Uncle Dave explained. "So it must be rainwater that filled in the lowland here, and besides, there hasn't been that much rain."

Reluctantly, Jake took off his sneakers and followed his uncle through the new marsh. He felt himself sinking deep into mud that sucked on his toes like quicksand.

"Move quickly and you won't get stuck," Uncle Dave coached.

Jake trudged through the muck, which reached almost to his ankles. He pushed thoughts of snakes and other slimy creatures from his mind. When he finally felt the grass and gravel base of the service road again, his heart was hammering. He took a moment to catch his breath.

"My house is just another 100 yards from here," Uncle Dave announced.

Relieved, Jake began to think about what a great story this would be to tell his friends. As he imagined telling his tale of bravery, he heard rustling in some nearby underbrush.

A stag with enormous antlers leapt onto the road and stopped in front of them. The stag stood as still as a mountain and looked Jake straight in the eyes.

The deer's stare didn't frighten Jake this time though. He stood tall. He realized he had nothing to fear anymore. He had made it through the crash, walked through the woods in the dark and rain, waded through the murky water with its muddied floor—and now they were almost home. He knew the deer wouldn't hurt him. And he knew that Uncle Dave would keep him safe until he was back with his parents again. He would have a lot to tell them too.

After a moment, the stag bounded off. The rest of the way home, Jake felt exhilarated by the night's events.

The opening in the clouds had grown, and the sky was now filled with stars and a bright moon. The porch light of his uncle's house was a beacon in the distance. He could see the outline of his parents' car. "I knew they'd be waiting," Uncle Dave said.

With their destination in sight, Jake and Uncle Dave picked up speed. Without a word, they started to race down the path to the finish.

Over steaming bowls of stew, Jake and Uncle Dave recounted the night's events to Jake's parents. They had been waiting in their car almost two hours. The first thing they said to Jake, after everyone had hugged, was, "We'll try never to miss one of your games again, son!"

Now Jake was saying, "There were wolves and coyotes. . . . Well, I never saw them, but I'm pretty sure. . . ."

"You must have been terrified!" said his mother.

"Yeah, at first I didn't know if I could make it," Jake replied.

"But he was really brave," Uncle Dave said with a proud smile.

Jake's dad was sitting back, nodding. Suddenly, he jumped up and offered high fives all around. Jake had never felt so proud in his life!

# Maine

Maine is located at the northeast tip of the United States. It is the largest New England state and ranks thirty-ninth in size in the nation.

Maine is famous for its beautiful landscape. Forests cover nearly 18 million acres of its 30,000 square miles. Its long coastline, stretching along the Atlantic Ocean, has both sandy and rocky beaches, bays, and coves. More than 2,000 islands dot Maine's coastal waters. The state also contains 6,000 lakes and ponds, numerous rivers and streams, and beautiful mountains. The tallest mountain is Mt. Katahdin, which is about one mile high.

Maine's attractions draw many tourists. They come to boat, fish, swim, hike, and ski. More than 25 ski areas are located in the state. Every autumn, Maine's highways fill with sightseers who come to enjoy the changing leaves. Maine proudly calls itself "Vacationland."